# Understanding
# Windows 98 Registry

# OTHER TITLES BY THE SAME AUTHOR

BP 418      Word 95 assistant

BP 421      Windows 95 assistant

BP 422      Essentials of computer security

BP 425      Microsoft Internet Explorer assistant

BP 427      Netscape Internet Navigator assistant

BP 434      PC hardware assistant

BP 437      Word 97 assistant

BP 438      Inside your PC

BP 439      Troubleshooting your PC

BP 446      How to get your PC up and running

BP 447      Multimedia explained

BP 449      Practical uses for your old PC

BP 451      Troubleshooting your PC printer

BP 454      Windows 98 assistant

BP 457      Windows 98 applets explained

BP 458      Tune up Windows 98

BP 463      Create your own Web site

# OTHER TITLES OF INTEREST

BP 455      Windows 98 – hard disc and file management

BP 456      Windows 98 explained

# Understanding Windows 98 Registry

by

Ian Sinclair

BERNARD BABANI (publishing) LTD
THE GRAMPIANS
SHEPHERDS BUSH ROAD
LONDON W6 7NF
ENGLAND

# PLEASE NOTE

Although every care has been taken with the production of this book to ensure that any projects, designs, modifications and/or programs, etc., contained herewith, operate in a correct and safe manner and also that any components specified are normally available in Great Britain, the Publishers and Author(s) do not accept responsibility in any way for the failure (including fault in design) of any project, design, modification or program to work correctly or to cause damage to any equipment that it may be connected to or used in conjunction with, or in respect of any other damage or injury that may be so caused, nor do the Publishers accept responsibility in any way for the failure to obtain specified components.

Notice is also given that if equipment that is still under warranty is modified in any way or used or connected with home-built equipment then that warranty may be void.

© 1999 BERNARD BABANI (publishing) LTD

First Published – May 1999


British Library Cataloguing in Publication Data:

A catalogue record for this book is available from the British Library

ISBN 0 85934 466.5


Cover Design by Gregor Arthur
Cover Illustration by Adam Willis
Printed and Bound in Great Britain by Bath Press, Bath

# PREFACE

Windows 98, like Windows 95, makes use of a database called the Registry to keep track of settings for Windows and for each program that you have installed on your computer. This task was formerly done by the INI files of Windows 3.1, but the INI system was clumsy and fragmented, and is available on Windows 95 and 98 only to ensure compatibility with older software. All information from INI files is converted into Registry entries when older software is installed on a modern PC system running Windows 98 (or 95).

The Registry, particularly in Windows 98, operates invisibly, and it is only when your computer locks up (often on the day following installation of some new software driver) that you suddenly realise that you owe so much to this set of files.

The fact that all the workings of Windows and the programs it runs are controlled by the Registry makes this database of utmost importance, so that you need to know how to make backups, how to restore a corrupted Registry, and how to maintain the Registry. This is not information that is readily available in Help files, and though Windows 98 has a good backup system for the Registry (unlike Windows 95), it is not explained in any detail.

The purpose of this book is to explain the Registry and how it is organised so that you can maintain backups, know how to restore a registry, and how to avoid problems caused by installation of software or disc corruption. Knowledge of the Registry is like insurance, you can work without it, but when anything happens you will be very glad that you have it.

This book is **NOT** recommended for beginners or those with little experience.

Ian Sinclair

Spring 1999

# ABOUT THE AUTHOR

Ian Sinclair was born in 1932 in Tayport, Fife, and graduated from the University of St. Andrews in 1956. In that year, he joined the English Electric Valve Co. in Chelmsford, Essex, to work on the design of specialised cathode-ray tubes, and later on small transmitting valves and TV transmitting tubes.

In 1966, he became an assistant lecturer at Hornchurch Technical College, and in 1967 joined the staff of Braintree College of F.E. as a lecturer. His first book, "Understanding Electronic Components" was published in 1972, and he has been writing ever since, particularly for the novice in Electronics or Computing. The interest in computing arose after seeing a Tandy TRS80 in San Francisco in 1977, and of his 180 published books, about half have been on computing topics, starting with a guide to Microsoft Basic on the TRS80 in 1979.

He left teaching in 1984 to concentrate entirely on writing, and has also gained experience in computer typesetting, particularly for mathematical texts. He has recently visited Seattle to see Microsoft at work, and to remind them that he has been using Microsoft products longer than most Microsoft employees can remember.

# ACKNOWLEDGEMENTS

I would like to thank the staff of Text 100 Ltd. for providing the Windows 98 software which is so frequently mentioned in the course of this book. I would also like to acknowledge the vast tank of useful information held on various Web sites and comments made in News group notes.

# TRADEMARKS

Microsoft, MS-DOS, Windows, Windows 95, Windows 98, Windows 2000, and NT are either registered trademarks or trademarks of Microsoft Corporation.

All other brand and product names used in this book are recognised as trademarks, or registered trademarks, of their respective companies.

# CONTENTS

**1 Know your Registry** ............................................................. 1

    Dire warning ............................................................................ 1

    What is the registry? .............................................................. 2

    The files .................................................................................... 3

    Registry content ..................................................................... 7

    The main sections .................................................................. 7

    Viewing the Registry ............................................................ 8

**2 Backing up** ............................................................................ 11

    Windows 98 tools ................................................................. 11

    The Scanreg utility ............................................................. 13

    The Scanreg.ini file ............................................................ 15

    CAB file contents ............................................................... 18

    Using REGEDIT .................................................................. 19

    Windows 95 differences ...................................................... 21

    Restoring a Windows 95 Registry ...................................... 22

    Windows 95 Registry utility .............................................. 25

**3 Problems and solutions** ..................................................... 27

    Old references ...................................................................... 27

    Manual methods .................................................................. 28

    Compacting utilities ........................................................... 29

    The RegClean action .......................................................... 32

    Third-party utilities ............................................................ 33

**4 Registry tweaks** .................................................................. 39

    Precautions ........................................................................... 39

    Registry editing ................................................................... 58

    Editing the Registry ............................................................ 59

    Some recommended tweaks ............................................... 63

    Default Search engine ......................................................... 63

    Download path ..................................................................... 64

    Multiple extensions ............................................................. 65

    Start menu speed ................................................................. 66

    Windows Setup path ........................................................... 66

**5 Disaster recovery** ........................................................**68**
  Don't panic! .............................................................68
  Corrupt backups ........................................................70

**Appendix A Sources for registry hints and tips**..............**72**

**Appendix B Other registry tools** ....................................**74**

**Appendix C Code numbers** ..............................................**75**

**INDEX**..................................................................................**76**

# 1 Know your Registry

---

## DIRE WARNING

**Before we start, you need to know that when you get into the business of editing your Registry you are on your own. The Registry can be altered using the Control Panel, the Policy Editor, or by using Microsoft software such as the Resources Kit. All of these methods are supported and you can get help if something goes wrong.**

**This book is NOT recommended for beginners or those with little experience!**

If you edit the Registry directly, using tools such as the *regedit* of Windows 98 (and in Windows 95) you must make a complete backup of the Registry in some spare folder before you make any alterations. If you do not, and the editing causes Registry problems you will have to sort it out for yourself, either by reversing your alterations or by restoring the Registry from the backup. Don't expect to be able to phone the Microsoft help-line, wait until *Greensleeves* is played for the forty-second time, and then get any assistance.

This warning applies also to installing new hardware or software. Practically all installation processes make alterations or additions to the Registry, and though installation is not quite such a hazard as editing the Registry it can cause problems. Once again, you should be certain that the Registry is backed up, even if the installation processes makes a backup (as it often does as part of an uninstall program).

- Windows 98 keeps an adequate number of backups automatically, but Windows 95 does not, and in either case you always ought to keep a fresh backup in a folder that is kept just for this purpose.

---

# Understanding Windows 98 Registry

> You should also know that there is an old utility called *regclean* that was originally written for Windows 95. The original version must not be run under Windows 98 (it usually refuses to run). A later version (4.1a) is noted in this book.
>
> This is the only full warning that I shall put in this book, because otherwise it becomes too repetitive. An incorrect Registry cannot be repaired unless you know what caused the fault or can use a backup. If a backup is too old, then it can cause problems with software that has been installed since the backup was made.

## What is the registry?

The Registry is a large and complicated database file that is created by Windows 98 when you install this system. The same system was used by Windows 95, and if you upgrade from Windows 95 to Windows 98, your Registry is transferred with all its entries (and any faults) during installation. Windows NT also uses the system, and the forthcoming Windows 2000, in all of its versions, will certainly follow the NT methods.

The entries in the file consist of data concerning the hardware, software, users, and preferences for a single PC with one or more users, or for any PC that is connected into a network. The Registry is altered when you make changes in the settings of the *Control Panel* or the *System Policies*, and when you create, delete or alter file associations.

In addition, when you install or remove any new software or upgrade existing software, this will also cause changes to be made to the Registry, though the changes are greater when you install new software than when you remove older software. Since this book is intended for the solo user, System Policies (for networked machines) are outside our remit.

- The Registry entries that are made when you install software are not necessarily totally removed when you de-install the software, even when you use the de-installation program that comes with the software. If you install and subsequently remove a large number of software items, which can easily happen if you try out time-limited programs from discs provided with magazines, your Registry can become very large, and this slows down the start and shutdown times for your computer.

The Registry system of Windows 95 and Windows 98 replaces the older system of .INI files that were used in Windows 3.1. The INI files were simple text files, using one line for each setup action, and the use by the Registry of a database type of structure allows for nesting (holding one folder inside another). This is a feature that, for example, allows several users access to a single PC, with each using a different setup. The other side of this coin is that if you are a user on a network, you can use any PC with the setup that you have on your own machine.

- Note that you will probably have INI files on your computer, because older software still uses these files, and Windows 98 has to maintain compatibility.

## The files

Windows NT uses a folder called:

Windows/System32/Config

to hold the Registry files, but both Windows 98 and Windows 95 contain the information in a pair of files called USER.DAT and SYSTEM.DAT. The Windows 98 files are large, around 3 Mbyte for SYSTEM.DAT and 500 Kbyte for USER.DAT, and no direct provision is made for saving them in a compressed form. The early version of Windows 95 used much smaller files that could be saved on a floppy, but the later (SR2 version) used larger files.

> In addition, Windows 95 had a pair of duplicate files called USER.DA0 and SYSTEM.DA0 (the 0 is zero, not letter *oh*) that could be renamed as a way of restoring a registry. This was not an ideal system, because it restored only the most recent previous settings (which might have the same faults as the files that were giving trouble), and because users who might have been brought up entirely on Windows needed to learn MS-DOS methods for renaming and changing attributes on the DA0 files.
>
> Though this book is devoted mainly to the Windows 98 Registry, we shall look at how to back up the Windows 95 Registry also.

Windows 98 uses a much improved Registry system, retaining the SYSTEM.DAT and USER.DAT files, and adding a POLICY.POL file if it is required (for several users of a single PC or for networked users). The larger file, SYSTEM.DAT is the one that contains all the information on installed hardware and software, plug and play settings, etc. The smaller USER.DAT file contains information that is specific to the user of the PC, such as log-on name, desktop settings, start menu settings and so on.

For a PC that has a single user, both of these files are stored in the C:\Windows folder, but if more than one user is provided for by way of a network or by using a *log on* system for each separate user of a single machine, the USER.DAT file will be held in the C:\Windows\Profiles folder. On a network, the USER.DAT file will be stored on the main server, and a SYSTEM.DAT file will be stored in the C:\Windows folder of each local machine. Other features of the Registry also allow for either the solo user or the sharing or networking of a machine.

- One point that sometimes puzzles users is that you can remove information from the Registry and yet see it reappear when you boot up next time. This is because there are still many software packages using INI and INF files, and these will be used if the data they carry is not contained in the Registry. In addition, the Registry is refreshed from these files. If you are utterly determined to remove a software item you have to remove all of its components. Look in particular at what is contained in your WIN.INI file.

Windows 98 performs a backup of the SYSTEM.DAT and USER.DAT files each *day* when you first boot up your PC, but the backup is not into DA0 files as it was for Windows 95. Instead, files are compressed using the system that Microsoft uses for distribution, into CAB files (using the CAB extension).

The default system is to use five CAB files stored in the

C:\Windows\sysbckup

folder, with the oldest of a set of five being replaced at each boot. This means that you should have five earlier Registry copies at any time, allowing you to choose one that you think will be good. The size of a CAB file is generally around 1 Mbyte, so that you can save it on a floppy. If your Registry grows so that the CAB files become larger than can be saved on a normally-formatted floppy, there are freeware or shareware programs that will carry out a special format to allow the storage of these larger files. If you need such a program for a bloated Registry, look in the Internet Web sites mentioned in the Appendices.

The reason for this multiple backing up is that two backups is not enough for real security. For example, suppose you boot up Windows 95 and the Registry is corrupted. This ought to cause an automatic start in *Safe Mode*, allowing you to recover the older Registry copy, but this does not always happen. If your computer starts and then locks up, the next boot will replace the Registry copy that you wanted to use with a copy of the corrupted one.

Using Windows 98, you can pick a copy that carries a date earlier than the time of the Registry corruption, so that you can restore a copy that you know ought to be good. This is particularly valuable if you know that all of your problems have started since you installed some software (usually a new driver).

These CAB files are normally located, as noted earlier, in the C:\Windows\Sysbckup folder, and they are named RB001.CAB to RB005.CAB. You may also find the file RBBAD.CAB which, as the name indicates, is the one that you have replaced and which should not be used. This is held in case a post-mortem is needed.

The method is good, but not infallible. Sometimes you find that there is something wrong with the operating system, but the Registry is not being replaced. This can continue until each CAB file copy bears the same fault, and you can also find that some CAB files will not restore your Registry — when you select a CAB file you get a message to the effect that no restoration is possible from that file so that you will be forced to select another. We shall look later at a way of increasing the number of backups into CAB files.

A faulty driver file or a conflict between drivers are the most likely reasons for this type of problem. The problem often shows up as a lockup, in which the pointer disappears and neither mouse nor keyboard has any effect, and you might not think right away that restoring the registry would be a cure.

As a further precaution, you should make a separate backup copy of the Registry at intervals, and certainly before you install new software. By separate, I mean avoiding the automatic system of CAB files and using the *Export* action to create a simple text backup file that can be placed in a folder and used to restore the Registry when necessary. There will be more of this later.

## Registry content

The Registry is built in layers (the form that we call a *hierarchical structure*) and you can think of this as being a set of folders within folders within folders..., for as great a depth as is needed. There are six main sections, sometimes called *hives*, and each section is devoted to a particular type of data. Each of these main sections contains a set of items called *keys*, and each key can have a value or set of values, or it can contain other keys which can have values or which can in turn contain further keys.

The keys are the names for bits of information, and the values attached to a key contain the information that is stored in the Registry. Some values can be numbers, and these are classed either as *binary* (small number) or as *Dword* (large number). Other values are names, and these are called *string* values. These names may be familiar to you if you have used a database or programmed in Basic.

## The main sections

The six main sections (or hives) of the Registry are listed below, along with brief comments of their use.

### HKEY_CLASSES_ROOT

This is the section that is used to store your file association types, OLE (embedding and linking) information, and shortcut data. Each time you make a new association of a file extension with a program, a new entry will be made here, but this set will also contain information for files and programs that you no longer use. The same is true of OLE information (allowing one file to be pasted into another) and shortcut information. The structure of this section consists of a large number of short entries of key and value items.

# Understanding Windows 98 Registry

## HKEY_CURRENT_USER

This is the section that contains the preferences for the current user. If several users share one PC, this set of keys will be the same as part of the HKEY_USERS section, but if there is only one user then this section is identical to HKEY_USERS.

## HKEY_LOCAL_MACHINE

is the section that contains all the information relating to your PC setup, its hardware, software and setting preferences. If more than one user logs on to this PC, then this information is available to all of them.

## HKEY_USERS

is the section that contains all the information specific to users. For one user, this is the same as the CURRENT_USER set, but if more than one user can log on, there is a separate portion (using a SID key) for each.

## HKEY_CURRENT_CONFIG

is a copy of the hardware information in the HKEY_LOCAL_MACHINE section.

## HKEY_DYN_DATA

is a copy of the Plug-and-Play information that is also contained in the LOCAL_MACHINE section. Each time you add or remove a piece of hardware, this section will be affected.

## Viewing the Registry

You can view the Registry by using a utility that is provided with both Windows 95 and Windows 98. This is *regedit*, and it is not installed into the set of programs that you reach from the Programs set in the Start menu. Instead, you have to call it up using the Start — Run command. You need to type the name *regedit* into the space provided and then click the *OK* button.

- *Regedit.exe* will also run under MS-DOS so that you can use it to restore a registry even if you cannot get Windows to start. This is a very useful point that is not sufficiently emphasised in Help pages.

Windows 95, and the earlier versions of Windows 98 (before Internet Explorer 5.0) retain all the items that you have typed into the Run box, so that once you have used *regedit* you do not have to type the name again — it will be available by clicking the arrowhead next to the entry panel of Run. The later version of Windows 98 clears this box each time you boot up, so that you need to type it again if you are using it in a new session. The change from storing the command seems to have been driven by the number of hints that were published about removing the stored list.

- If you are likely to use *regedit* frequently, you can make a shortcut to the file which is held in the C:\Windows folder. This saves having to use the Start button and type the name in the *Run* space.

When you run *regedit* you will see the Registry data displayed in two panes set side by side. The left side shows the six main sections as sub-folders of *My Computer*. For each section, clicking the [+] symbol at the left of the hive name will display a set of keys for that section, and if a key also has the [+] symbol next to it this indicates a further sub-key.

Clicking on a key will bring up, in the right-hand pane, the data that is associated with that key. A typical data entry will consist of three parts, the name, the data type and the data value. The editor provides for deleting or adding a key, and for changing name, type or values, so that you can put in new entries, delete old entries, or change values.

## Understanding Windows 98 Registry

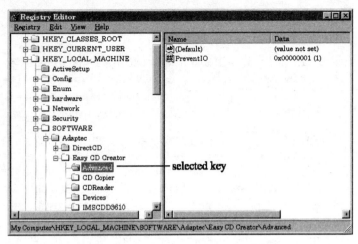

This is what makes the warnings about backing up a registry so important. If you try to create a new key using a name that is not acceptable, or you alter the type or value to something impossible or conflicting, then you risk locking up your computer. If this happens, you will have to reboot, and the computer should then start in safe mode, allowing you only minimal use of essential software until the fault is cured by restoring the Registry.

# 2 Backing up

## Windows 98 tools

Users of Windows 98 have a considerable advantage over users of Windows 95 in terms of the automatic backing up of the Registry files. The downside of this is that the action of checking and backing up adds considerably to the time needed for booting up. If you are prepared to save registry files manually, the boot time for your computer can be greatly reduced, but you are definitely on your own if you suffer from a Registry fault.

The main tool for Registry backup in Windows 98 is the one that also provides the automatic action, *Registry Checker*, which was not used on Windows 95. The *Registry Checker* is responsible for the automatic action of backing up the Registry data at most once a day (not each time you boot in a day).

- The automatic backup action also extends to the SYSTEM.INI and WIN.INI files, because these contain data that is copied into the Registry for older software.

As we noted earlier, the Registry backups are compressed into compressed CAB files and stored in the folder C:\Windows\Sysbackup. These CAB files are generally small enough to fit onto a floppy, and you can copy one to a floppy now and again as a further backup. This has the advantage of providing a backup that does not depend on the hard drive (or on a CD-ROM).

Note that the backups you can make using the *Export* command of *regedit* are text files that are much too large to fit on a conventional floppy, though you can use any of the Zip (™)compression programs to make a file that will easily fit on a floppy. You can also use Microsoft Backup on Windows 98 to ensure that the Registry is backed up along with other files that you specify.

You can, however, use *Registry Checker* manually, though it is well hidden in your Windows 98 files. To find this utility, click in turn on Start, Programs, Tools, System Information to get to the *System Information* panel. When you see this panel, click on its Tools menu, and then on *Registry Checker*. This will check the Registry, report the results, and give you a chance to make another backup if you want (the automatic system makes just one new backup each day, remember).

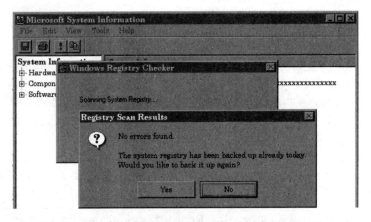

- Don't be fooled by *Registry Checker*. All it can do is to check if the entries look convincing, with permitted names and values. It is quite possible that a Registry entry that obeys the rules is nevertheless a cause of trouble, and in that event the *Registry Checker* will happily accept it. There are some software packages that are more rigorous, and these will try to match the Registry entries with the software that they refer to, so that unused items can be weeded out. There is no absolutely foolproof way of finding an entry that looks right but which is the cause of trouble.

## The Scanreg utility

When Windows 98 is installed, two versions of a Registry scanning utility are placed on your hard drive. One is a Windows utility called **SCANREGW.EXE**, placed in the C:\Windows folder, and this simply carries out the actions of the Registry Checker without the need to go through all the menu steps. SCANREGW is usually executed in the form:

### SCANREGW /autoscan

which forces an inspection of the Registry files followed by a backup action. The Registry files will also be compacted (*optimised*) if the scan finds a large amount of unused space.

The other utility is a DOS tool called **SCANREG.EXE**, located in the C:\Windows\Command folder and some of its actions can be obtained using the MS-DOS prompt of Windows to run the program (do not try to use it from the Start — Run menu item).

The **SCANREG** utility is particularly useful if you cannot start Windows, and you should know how to use it. If you are not familiar with MS-DOS (only we old-timers remember MS-DOS these days) then you should try out the actions when your computer is still healthy so that you know what to do when (**not** if) things go wrong.

- Let's put that into perspective. The only time I have ever had to restore a Registry manually is after suffering lockups following installation of a driver for a trackball. Usually a de-installation of the driver would have been enough, but in this case only a Registry restore had any effect. This is why I have emphasised the importance of making a Registry backup before installing any hardware with new drivers.

## Understanding Windows 98 Registry

SCANREG can be run from the MS-DOS prompt from within Windows, but the restore action of SCANREG can only be used from MS-DOS when Windows is shut down and not running — you will be reminded of this if you try to restore while you are running Windows.

This is because problems will arise if a Registry is changed while Windows is still using it. If a severe problem with the Registry is found during the booting action it will cause the machine to open with the menu choice that allows you to go immediately to MS-DOS (Command mode) without running Windows. This is the same menu as you see when you start the machine with the F8 or the left-hand Ctrl key held down.

By taking the *Command Prompt* option from this menu, you can get to the MS-DOS screen, and you can type:

SCANREG /?

to see the list of SCANREG options — note that there must be a space between the letter G and the slash sign. The options appear as follows:

SCANREG /backup

This will immediately make another backup of the registry and associated files. The same action is obtained from within Windows by using SCANREGW

SCANREG /restore

This will show you a list of the backup files that are available as CAB files in the C:\Windows\Sysbckup folder, with the date and time shown for each backup. When you select a CAB file you can carry out a restoration from it, and the Registry that you are replacing will be stored under the filename of RBBAD.CAB.

SCANREG /COMMENT ="comment"

Allows you to make a comment on a backup — the comment is placed between quotes, so that you might, for example, use SCANREG /backup /COMMENT="doubtful" for a backup you could not be sure of.

### SCANREG /fix

Will attempt to carry out repairs on Registry files. This may repair some types of fault, but you cannot rely on this to the extent that you could abandon backups.

### SCANREG /scanonly

This will check through, but not back up, the Registry files, and displays a number that indicates any errors. The numbers that can appear are:

2     meaning that the Registry is corrupted and should not be used. There is no point in making a backup of a corrupted Registry.

0     meaning that no problems were found.

-2     meaning that there was not enough memory available to MS-DOS to complete the action. MS-DOS can use only the first 640 Kbyte of memory, so that a machine with 32 Mbyte of RAM still has only 640 Kbyte available to MS-DOS. A small amount of additional memory can be made available is HIMEM.SYS is used in the CONFIG.SYS file

-3     meaning that one or both of the Registry files cannot be found. You will need to restore files from the CAB set.

-4     meaning that Registry files cannot be created. This indicates some deep-seated fault in the system, and there is no simple solution.

## The Scanreg.ini file

The actions of SCANREG and SCANREGW are set up by the file called SCANREG.INI, which is located in the C:\Windows folder. This is a plain text file, like all other INI files, and it can be edited in Windows *Notepad*. Once you have changed this file all subsequent backups will follow the pattern dictated by the altered INI file.

The SCANREG.INI file is arranged to guide you through any alterations. Any line that starts with the semicolon (;) is a comment line, and is not any form of command, so that the file contains its own Help system. For example, the first three lines are:

```
;
; Scanreg.ini for making system backups.
;
```

used to announce that this is the correct file for Scanreg.ini

The first command line is:

Backup=1

with no space on either side of the equality sign. This line commands a Registry backup, and if the 1 is changed to a zero then the backup action will not be performed by SCANREG or SCANREGW, only the scanning action will be done.

The next active line is:

Optimize=1

to ensure that the Registry is compacted if there is too much free space. This compacting will be omitted if you edit the INI file and change the 1 to 0.

The line

ScanregVersion=0.0001

must not be altered, but this is followed by:

MaxBackupCopies=5

in which the number can be altered. You can, for example, change the figure 5 to 10 so that ten CAB files are maintained, ensuring that ten days of previous Registry settings are available in the CAB files. I cannot think of any good reason for reducing the number from the default of five, however.

The following line is:

BackupDirectory=

and the blank space following the equality sign allows you to type in the name of a folder in which the CAB files can be stored. The default is C:\Windows\Sysbckup, but this will be overruled if you type in a value for BackupDirectory. If you use this option, you must type a full folder path starting from C:\, such as C:\precious\CAB_file.

- In case you have to locate this folder using MS-DOS, it's better to use a filename that follows DOS 8-3 naming conventions rather than the longer filename type you can use in Windows. If you use a long name it will appear abbreviated when you are using MS-DOS, and you may not recognise it.

You can add a last line to the SCANREG.INI file if you want to specify other files that you want added into the CAB files. The SYSTEM.INI and WIN.INI files are backed up by default, and other files can be added by a command line that starts with:

FILES=

and contains a folder code and a list of files separated by commas. The folder code is used to specify the folder that is used to store the files you want to back up, and the permitted numbers are:

10 Windows folder

11 Windows/System folder

30 Boot folder C:\

31 Boot host folder (usually C:\)

17

## Understanding Windows 98 Registry

For example, if you wanted to add the MSDOS.SYS file (usually stored in C:\) to your backup you would use the line:

FILES=30,msdos.sys

and you can add other filenames, separated by command, following this on. For example, if you needed to keep copies of Autoexec.bat and Config.sys, you could use:

FILES=30,msdos.sys,autoexec.bat,config.sys

You can, in fact, specify a full folder path in place of the number code if you want to. For example, you might use:

Files=C:\Program Files\Microsoft Office\Templates\Normal.dot

to ensure that a copy of the Word *Normal* template was made on each backup. This is not really needed because Word makes its own backups, but it makes a good example.

## CAB file contents

You may have read that it is not possible to check the contents of a CAB file. Though this was true of Windows 95, Windows 98 makes it possible simply by locating the file in Explorer and clicking on it. When you do this, you will see a panel open with a list of the files contained in the CAB file.

This is presented in the standard Internet Explorer format, and some of the CAB files on the distribution disc contain a very large number of files so that scrolling is needed if you want to see the whole set. You may have to use the Find action if you are looking for a specific file.

As the illustration shows, you can opt for display of the CAB files in the usual ways, as icons, as a list, or with more details. What is not brought out in the illustration is that the File menu contains only *Work offline* and *Close* until you select a file, at which point the *Extract* item appears in the File menu.

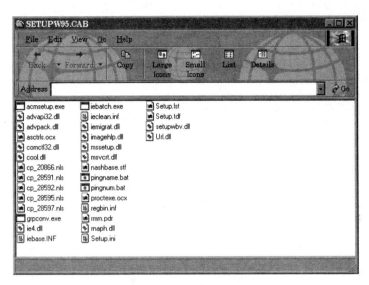

Any file or set of files can be selected, and you will find an *Extract* command in the Files menu, allowing you to extract files from the CAB folder into any folders you want to use. You can also use the *Copy* command to copy the file to the Clipboard to be pasted in anywhere you want.

## Using REGEDIT

The regedit utility can also be used for backing up manually, and this is something that is often neglected. The backup takes the form of a very large text file which can be edited as a way of altering the registry. This file can be compressed by using, for example, WinZip, so that it can be saved on a floppy.

To make a backup of the complete Registry, start regedit by using Start — Run and typing or selecting the name, then clicking the *OK* button. When regedit starts, it will show the Registry with the name *My Computer* selected, and this permits a backup of the whole registry. If you select a section, such as HKEY_LOCAL_MACHINE, then only this portion of the Registry will be saved.

## Understanding Windows 98 Registry

Now open the File menu and click on *Backup*. You will see a folder tree so that you can specify a location (by default this will be on the C: drive) for storing the backup files, and you should type a filename that reminds you when the backup was made. For example, I use a format such as *REG9_2_99* to show the date.

When you click on *OK* for this the backup will be made, saving the file with the extension letters of **reg**. This backup can subsequently be restored by using File — Restore and locating the *reg* file that you want to restore, using the date as a guide to the most recent good file you backed up.

This system can be very useful because it is entirely manual, so that there is no chance that you could work through all of the backups substituting bad files for good. In fact, if you were well enough organised you could make all of your backups in this way rather than using the automatic system (by setting Backup=0 in the SCANREG.INI file). System booting would then be faster because you have eliminated the time needed for making the backups.

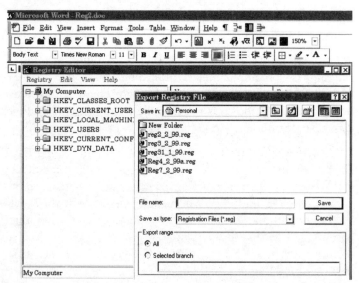

## Windows 95 differences

Registry backup using Windows 95 was, as we have indicated, much more primitive, using only the DA0 files as backups. On each boot (**not** on the first boot of each day), the DAT files will be copied as DA0 files, and then used as the Registry. The trouble with this simple scheme is that if you reboot after the system has crashed with a Registry fault, and the system crashed again, you will be backing up with files that are already faulty.

There are two ways round this. One is the obvious method of making additional copies of USER.DAT and SYSTEM.DAT for yourself, placing them in a folder that is not otherwise used and making new backups at intervals, particularly just before installing new hardware or software.

If no other copies of the Registry files are available, you can make use of a hidden file called SYSTEM.1ST (the extension starts with the numeral one, not the letter I). This file contains the first working Registry settings that Windows 95 created when it was installed, and a version of this file is also created when you install Windows 98.

The SYSTEM.1ST file is not used again after Windows has been run for the first time, so that it contains the original Registry settings, with no entries for any hardware or software that has been installed since the date that you will find in the Properties for the file.

- This means that you might have to reinstall a large number of software and hardware items to get back to the state you had before a Registry corruption, but if you do not have any good backups that's all you can do. It's certainly preferable to re-installing the whole of Windows.

## Understanding Windows 98 Registry

## Restoring a Windows 95 Registry

Many of the methods that are illustrated in the following section will work on Windows 98 (allowing for the point that there are no DA0 files in Windows 98), but because Windows 98 allows so many other and easier ways of recovery we generally use these methods on Windows 95 only.

- The restoration of a Windows 95 Registry is hard work, but if you are familiar with MS-DOS it's not all that difficult. The trouble is that you may be learning to cope with MS-DOS and with restoration at the same time, and that's considerably more difficult.

When you boot your computer with a corrupted Registry, Windows will start in *safe* mode. This is a restricted form of Windows that uses the absolute minimum of drivers. The video will be set to VGA 640 × 480, and the Microsoft mouse driver will be used.

You cannot make use of other peripherals that use drivers, such as printers, CD-ROM, scanners, etc., in safe mode, nor can you run software applications other than *regedit*. All that you can do is to change some settings using the *Control Panel*, *Network*, or *System* items. If the problem lies in these sections, then you can sort it out (usually by removing a driver) and you will be able to restart Windows normally when you reboot.

If the fault has been in a setting that you can change while the machine is working in safe mode, all and well, but more usually you will find that this will not cure the problem. You must then start in MS-DOS command mode, booting with the F8 or left-hand Ctrl key held down so that you see the boot-options menu appear. The best option is the one labelled as *safe mode command prompt only*, and selecting this puts you into MS-DOS with a set of defaults operating.

- In MS-DOS you may find that some keys on your keyboard do not perform as you expect. For example, you may find the " and @ keys interchanged. This is most likely to happen if you work only with Windows and do not use the CONFIG.SYS and AUTOEXEC.BAT files.

To start with, you have a very good chance of making a simple restoration if the backup DA0 files are good. If Windows cannot find the SYSTEM.DAT file it will use the SYSTEM.DA0 one, and one method of getting back into Windows is to delete or change the extension name of SYSTEM.DAT. Simply deleting is the easier option, but can be fraught. What do you do if nothing works after deleting the file?

The problem is that you are now working under MS-DOS, and the SYSTEM.DAT file is hidden and read-only under MS-DOS, no matter what you have specified under Windows. You need to remove the system, hidden and read-only attributes from the file so that you can rename it.

If, as often happens, you are in the C:\ folder and running MS-DOS, get to the C:\Windows folder by typing:

CD C:\windows

— pressing the Return key to execute the command, as you must for each MS-DOS command line. Now type:

ATTRIB –s –h –r SYSTEM.DAT

and press Return, so that the attributes are changed. You can now type:

REN SYSTEM.DAT SYSTEM.BAD

and press Return again to rename the file as SYSTEM.BAD. Now you can close down, and reboot. This time, Windows should make use of the SYSTEM.DA0 file, renaming it as SYSTEM.DAT, and you should see Windows start.

## Understanding Windows 98 Registry

Another way is to get into MS-DOS command mode as before, and change to the C:\Windows folder by using:

```
CD C:\Windows
```

and pressing the Return key. Now carry out the following set of DOS commands, remembering to press the Return key at the end of each line:

```
attrib -h -r -s system.dat

attrib -h -r -s system.da0

copy system.da0 system.dat

attrib -h -r -s user.dat

attrib -h -r -s user.da0

copy user.da0 user.dat
```

all of which will remove the hidden, system and read-only attributes and copy the files. You might want to restore the attributes later, once you have everything working again, using the lines from MS-DOS:

```
attrib h r s system.dat

attrib h r s user.dat
```

Now you can reboot with reasonable confidence that all will be well.

- If the DA0 files are also corrupted, then in the absence of other backups you will have to use the SYSTEM.1ST method that we noted earlier.

This also uses MS-DOS methods, and the steps are listed here, this time without the reminder to press the Return key at the end of each line.

```
CD C:\Windows

ATTRIB -h -r -s SYSTEM.DAT

REN SYSTEM.DAT SYSTEM.BAD
```

CD C:\

ATTRIB –h –r –s SYSTEM.1ST

COPY SYSTEM.1ST C:\Windows\SYSTEM.DAT

ATTRIB h r s SYSTEM.1ST

This set of instructions selects the C:\Windows folder and then removes the attributes from the SYSTEM.DAT file so that it can be renamed. This done, we shift to the C:\ folder to find the SYSTEM.1ST file and remove its attributes. This file is then copied to the \Windows folder as the new SYSTEM.DAT, and the protective attributes are then re-applied.

Remember that this restores the Registry to the form it had when Windows 95 was first installed — it is the equivalent (though much quicker) of installing Windows 95 again with the software that you had at that date. Software or hardware that you installed later than this time will now have to be reinstalled.

## Windows 95 Registry utility

Windows 95 does not have the automatic system for making multiple backups that is present in Windows 98, but there is a utility that can do this manually, and if you are not intending to move to Windows 98 fairly soon you should make full use of it.

The utility is called CFGBACK.EXE, and it should be on your Windows 95 CD-ROM disc in the Other\Misc\Cfgback folder. You can copy the backup utility and its help file on to your hard drive and make use of it from there. Alternatively, you can hold the EXE file on a floppy disc.

When you run CFGBACK.EXE you can opt for backup or restore actions. The backup tool will save the Windows 95 registry as a file called REGBACK1.RBK, and subsequent backups can be made using numbers 2 to 9. When you restore, you can choose which version to restore from. This is, in fact, the ancestor of the system that is used in Windows 98.

The snag is that CFGBACK.EXE cannot be run from Windows in safe mode, and another utility, ERU, is better in this respect. The ERU (emergency recovery unit) is also on the Windows 95 CD-ROM, in the Other\Misc\ERU folder. When you double-click on the ERU icon, it allows you to save your Windows 95 registry to a floppy together with a file called ERD.EXE. To restore the Registry, boot into MS-DOS, and use the command:

A:\ERD.EXE

You should make a new backup each time before and after you add hardware or software.

Ideally, you should use both ERU and CFGBACK for backups, not relying entirely on the DA0 files.

# 3 Problems and solutions

## Old references

One major problem concerning the Windows 98 Registry is that the file grows enormously as you use your computer. The Windows 98 Registry does not have the same limitations on size as the Windows 95 version (which allowed a maximum key size of 64 Kbyte), so it takes up several Mbytes when Windows 98 is first installed, and it can grow well beyond this.

- Much of this size may not be needed. If you are continually installing and then removing programs, the main files of these programs may be removed, but the Registry entries may not, so that your Registry is likely to be cluttered with references to hardware drivers and software applications that are no longer held anywhere else on your hard drive. This leads to a bloated Registry that causes long boot times. Some uninstall programs clean up the Registry, but others do not.

In addition, the Registry often incorporates empty spaces, and though Windows 98 will automatically compact the Registry now and again it is useful to know how this can be done when you want it (such as just before you do a defragmentation run).

Both manual and automatic methods exist, and we'll start by looking at the manual methods, because you will need to download software (or look for alternative sources from providers of shareware) for some of the utilities that will carry out the tasks for you.

## Understanding Windows 98 Registry

## Manual methods

When you remove an application you will normally use the Control Panel option of *Add/Remove programs*, though older software will not appear on the *Remove* list. For such older software you will have to remove the files manually. This is easy enough if all the files are in one folder, but there may be others scattered around the system, and some files will be shared (so that they cannot be deleted without causing problems with other software). The sharing of library files, the ones with the DLL extension, is one of the most potent causes of trouble when you add or remove software.

Whatever method you use to remove the obvious files, you will usually find that the Registry is unaffected, so that if you have removed a number of programs and hardware, the Registry will still hold details. This clutters up the Registry, and one way to clean it out is to go through it with *regedit* and remove references manually. Do I need to add that you would make a backup first?

This is tedious, but not as bad as it sounds. *Regedit* has a *Find* facility, obtained from the Edit menu. If you fill in the name of the program that you have just deleted, you can find the first reference to it, and by pressing the F3 key you will find the next reference and so on.

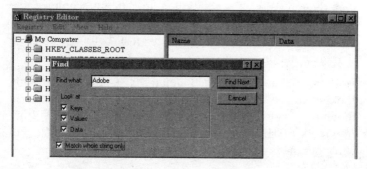

If you are certain that these are genuine references to this program you can delete them, using the Del key or the Edit — Delete menu command.

- You can also use the *Find* system to look for extension letters for programs that you have deleted.

It's not so easy if you have deleted a number of programs but not updated the Registry. You may not have a note of exactly what you have deleted, and so you will have to look at the Registry with *regedit*, concentrating on the Software section of HKEY_LOCAL_MACHINE. This is where items such as program installation information, registration information and version information will be held.

- If you are using a shared PC, the user names are held in HKEY_USERS, and you can delete a user from the system by editing this part of the database.

## Compacting utilities

There are a few utilities that can be obtained for working on the Windows 98 Registry, and these are obtained by downloading, though some shareware sources may keep copies. The most important is REGCLEAN 4.1a, which is a Microsoft product, though at the time of writing it is not fully supported.

Beware of earlier versions! Version 4.1 will not run under Windows 98, and would probably cause problems if it did. Versions earlier than 4.1 should **not** be used unless you know what you are doing and you are using an early version of Windows 95. If you get a message about a file called OLEAUT32.DLL:421 then you should abandon the use of RegClean 4.1a.

The current version in February 1999 is labelled as Version 4.1a build 7364.1. This can be downloaded free of charge from the FTP site:

29

## Understanding Windows 98 Registry

ftp://ftp.microsoft.com/softlib/MSLFILES/regclean.exe

and you can make a shortcut to it in the usual way so that you can start it by clicking on an icon or by selection from a list.

When you start *RegClean* you will see a message about the *RegClean* action, and while you are reading this message the Registry checking action runs. There is currently no option to read the message and then not to proceed. The checking actions are signalled briefly along with a progress meter (a horizontal bar display) on the lower portion of the panel. Once the Registry has been checked, an action that does not make any changes in the Registry, you can opt to continue by clicking a *Fix errors* button, or to abandon the cleaning action by clicking the *Cancel* button.

- Future versions may allow a pause before checking, because the greyed-out buttons on the panel show options of *Start* and *Cancel*.

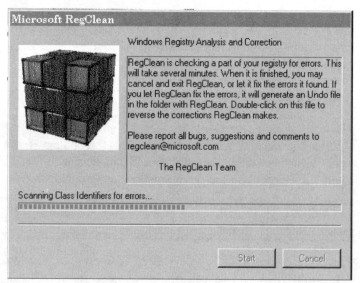

If your Registry is really in a mess, the checking will take some time, and it can sometimes seem to halt for a while. By contrast, if your Registry is well-organised, the checking will be completed by the time you have finished reading the notice. Obviously, the time required depends on the processor speed as well.

If the checking is completed, and the *Fix errors* button is greyed out, there are no errors in your Registry, and you can leave *RegClean*. If there are errors, you can click the button to fix them, or click *Cancel* to escape if you do not want your Registry changed.

When errors have been reported and you click the *Fix errors* button, another progress meter will indicate how far *RegClean* has gone. For a well-maintained Registry this stage may be over in the twinkling of an eye, but for a Registry that has suffered a large amount of installing and deletion of programs without any effort to remove unwanted entries, the fixing stage may take several seconds and can sometimes look as if it has stalled. Once the bar display disappears you can click on the *Exit* button to shut down RegClean.

The *Fix errors* action will create an *Undo* file, so that if you wanted to restore your Registry to the state it was in before running *RegClean* you can do so. The *Undo* file is placed in the same folder as *regclean.exe*, and consists of a line such as:

Undo MESH 1990210 095406.reg

which consists of the word *Undo* followed by the name of your computer, the date, and then the time of the Registry cleaning action. The name of your Internet provider may be used rather than the name of the computer. The file is not a backup for the entire Registry, only for the items that were judged by *RegClean* to be faulty, so that the *Undo* files are usually quite small, typically 2 Kbyte or so.

# Understanding Windows 98 Registry

You can click this *Undo* filename to restore the Registry to its previous dirty condition. You will be asked to confirm that you really want to restore the items in this file

- Keep your *Undo* files because you might not be aware from some time if a *RegClean* action has caused problems. If only a few errors have been found, the *Undo* file will be short and can easily be fitted on a floppy.

## The RegClean action

*Regclean* checks each key in each location of the Registry, looking for keys whose value is incorrect and recording the key and value entries in the *Undo* file. When you opt not to fix errors, this file is deleted, but if you opt to fix the errors the file is stored and the Registry keys and values are deleted instead.

- This is a maintenance action only, and *RegClean* does not alter incorrect values such as might have been caused by corruption.

If your computer has been showing signs of Registry problems (such as hanging up for no apparent reason), then you cannot rely on *RegClean* to provide a solution — it is usually better to restore the Registry using a copy that was made before the problems started. In particular, *RegClean* will never remove a Registry entry that is of the correct format, because it has no way of distinguishing between a good entry and a bad entry if both appear correctly formatted. *RegClean* will also make no changes to an entry that is of a pattern that is unfamiliar.

If you find that you have problems in using other programs (particularly Network Viewer) after running *RegClean* then you should restore the Registry from the *Undo* file and wait for an update to *RegClean* before you try to use it again.

A minor problem which is not strictly a *RegClean* problem, is that clicking on the *Undo* file may have no effect. This will happen if the *reg* extension is not associated with the *regedit.exe* program, and this is possible if you have never used *regedit.exe* to export registry (*reg*) files.

The remedy is to carry out the association as follows:

1.  Open Explorer and click View, then select Options — File Types.

2.  Look on the list of types for the entry called *Registration Entries*. Click on this so that the panel labelled *Edit File Type* appears. There should be an entry called *Merge*. Click on this item.

3.  Now click the *Edit* button. Another smaller panel will open with a section labelled *Application used to perform action*. The entry in this panel should be:

    regedit.exe "%1"

    and if this is not present you will need to type this line. You can then click your way out of the panels, and once you have done so, clicking an *Undo* file should bring up the confirmation message panel allowing you to start the action.

### Third-party utilities

The fact that *RegClean* is not (yet) officially supported by Microsoft, and the problems that arose with early versions led to several other Registry utilities being devised and launched, many of them shareware. None of these will solve all the problems of a corrupted Registry, and ideally you should use more than one utility at intervals. One that comes more strongly recommended than others, however, is *Perfect Companion*.

This software can be downloaded from the site:

http://members.aol.com/qikneasy/perfect.htm

and it is limited to a trial period of ten days, after which you will need to register and pay if you want to continue using your downloaded copy. The download is of about 1622 Kbyte and is reasonably fast if you are using a 34K or 56K modem.

You are reminded when you visit the site that *Perfect Companion* makes use of *Visual Basic* routines, and some VB5 supporting files are needed. These will already be on your computer if you have downloaded and used other programs written in Visual Basic, but if they are not they can be downloaded and used free of charge.

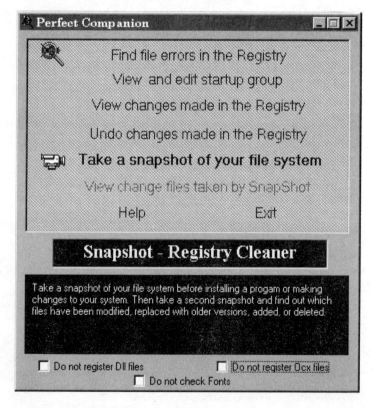

# Problems and solutions

The recommended way of using *Perfect Companion* is to use its *Snapshot* facility, a form of backup, before installing or un-installing a piece of new software, and follow this action with the Registry cleaner utility if any problems show up.

The *Snapshot* utility will read and log all of the files on your hard drive or you can opt to confine this to the Windows folder, or to extend it to other drives. The *Perfect Companion* control panel will remain on your screen in the foreground even if you switch to other programs while it is working. The log files that it creates are stored in the same folder as your other *Perfect Companion* files using the name *filelog.dat.*

When you have made changes to your system, including installing or removing software or hardware, you can then take a second Snapshot. This allows you to use the option titled:

View change files taken by Snapshot

so that you can see a list of which files have been replaced with older versions or modified during an installation. This is particularly important because library files, the files with the DLL extensions, are often shared by several applications, and when a new piece of software replaces one DLL file by a new version it may cause problems.

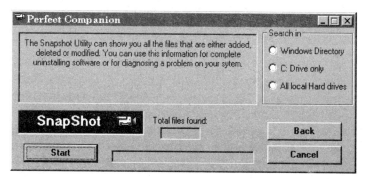

# Understanding Windows 98 Registry

This *change files* option will also show which files have been added to or deleted from your system. It will not remove any files that may have been added during an installation. If you have used an uninstall utility belonging to a program, this will have deleted the main files of that program, but not all traces of the program. *Snapshot* can then be used to locate and remove these traces, particularly DLL files that are not shared by other applications.

The other options of *Perfect Companion* concern the *Start* set and the Registry. The *Startup* group is a set of programs that are launched along with Windows, and unless you are using a portable machine you can usually dispense with the item called SYSTRAY.EXE. You will lose the loudspeaker icon for quick access to the volume control, but if you do not use sound this is no great loss. The change can be done by using the *Delete entry* button when you are using the *Start* group editor, but you can also remove SYSTRAY.EXE in a more reversible way by using the *Windows 98 System Information* tools

The portion of *Perfect Companion* that deals with the Registry consists of the three options:

Find file errors in the Registry

View changes made in the Registry

Undo changes made in Registry

and the actions are obvious from the titles.

When you click the *Find file errors* option this will start Perfect Companion scanning the Registry looking for items such as keys that do not correspond to stored programs, or other references to material that has been deleted. In this time you will see reports appearing to tell you which section of the Registry is being scanned, as the illustration shows.

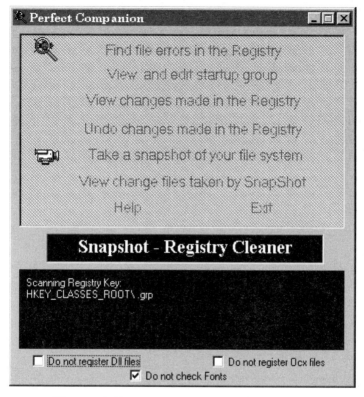

- The *Find file errors* action will remove any Registry entry that is not valid. It will remove a key whose entry contains an incorrect path or an invalid quotation mark, comma, period, backslash, or any other invalid character.

Each time the *file errors* option is used, an *Undo* file called *PcUndo.reg* will be created, and any older *Undo* file will be deleted. This file is located in the C:\Windows\System folder. The file errors option will also repair any faults it finds in the *Fonts* folder and the *Recycle bin* when the machine is booted following a Registry clean.

# Understanding Windows 98 Registry

- You can opt to omit *Fonts* checking, or the registration of DLL or OCX files by ticking the appropriate box in the Perfect Companion *file errors* panel.

# 4 Registry tweaks

## Precautions

Registry tweaking means editing the Registry to alter some feature of your system, and you are recommended to do such tweaking, if at all possible, by way of the normal Windows 98 Control Panel or by using the Windows Resources Sampler Kit in the Windows 98 distribution CD-ROM. These are by far the simplest and most foolproof ways of carrying out Registry alterations. They cannot, however, carry out all the possible Registry alterations that you might want.

The **setup** program of the *Sampler* collection is loacted in the folder:

D:\Tools\Reskit

assuming your CD-ROM drive is lettered D, and it can be used to create a folder called WIN98RK containing the files. In addition, a Control Panel item called *TweakUI* will be created to allow you to make use of desktop modifications under the headings of *Mouse*, *General*, *Explorer*, *IE4*, *Desktop*, *My Computer*, *Control Panel*, *Network*, *New*, *Add/Remove*, *Boot*, *Repair*, and *Paranoia*. When you view this set initially you will see only the first six items, and you have to scroll by clicking on the arrowheads to see the others.

- Some tweaks can interfere with other software. In particular, you may find that if you are not using the standard Microsoft mouse driver the tweaks in the Mouse section of TweakUI may cause problems that can only be repaired by restoring an older version of the Registry.

## Understanding Windows 98 Registry

- Note that some changes may have unexpected results on some of your programs. Always make changes one at a time, and keep a note of what you have done.

- The panels that appear all have the **?** icon for selective Help, but this has no effect for some of the items. Instead, you should right-click on an item and then click on the *What's This* menu item that appears at the pointer.

### Mouse

This tab deals with the way that the mouse works. It can, for example, determine the speed at which a cascading menu, meaning a menu that leads to another menu, will open up when you move the mouse over each cascading menu item. The fastest setting will cause these menus to open immediately. The slowest setting is very slow, giving you plenty time for second thoughts.

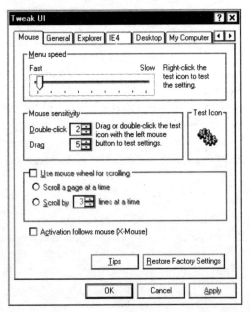

- If you share your computer, each user can log on and can make different individual settings for the mouse.

The portion that deals with *double-click sensitivity* is not so important for Windows 98 as it was for Windows 95. This is not a matter of how **fast** you click (which is dealt with in the *Mouse* item of Control Panel) but the distance the pointer can be moved between clicks. If the pointer is moved between two clicks, these can be interpreted as two separate clicks, and it can be useful to make this distance large if you are likely to move the mouse between clicks. The distance is specified in pixels (screen points) and the default is 2 pixels.

The *drag sensitivity* item is useful if you find that you often drag objects accidentally when you are really just clicking. Once again, you have to specify how many pixels of movement have to be made before the computer takes this as a dragging action. The default is 2 pixels, and many users will want to increase this.

You can test both of these sensitivity settings by clicking on the icon of the gearwheels. Click twice with the pointer moving to see if the image changes, and decide if you want to alter the double-click setting. You can then try dragging, and see how far the pointer can move before the drag action starts. Once again, if you share your computer, each logged user can make his/her own settings.

The next item applies only if you have a mouse, such as the *Intellimouse*, that incorporates a scrolling wheel. If you check the *Use mouse wheel for scrolling* box this will allow the use of the mouse wheel to scroll data. With this enabled you can choose the amount of scrolling as a page or a specified number of lines (such as the number of lines per screen view). Once again, each logged-on user can make individual settings.

The last main item on the Mouse panel is a checkbox labelled *Activation follows mouse (X-mouse)*, and this can be ticked if you want your mouse to behave in this way. Normally, when your screen shows several windows, you activate a window by placing the mouse pointer over it and clicking. *X-Mouse* behaviour eliminates the need to click, so that whatever window your mouse pointer is over becomes the active window. This choice also is available separately to each different user of your computer. If the *X-Mouse* item is greyed you will need to find and use the *Xmouse* Power Toy item.

- Using this option can have odd effects on programs that have a pop-down action. For example, Quicken accounts uses a popdown calendar and calculator facility that will no longer work if the *X-mouse* option is used. Many users prefer to dispense with X-mouse action.

For each item on the Mouse panel you can click the *Apply* button to make the action operative, and the button marked *Restore Factory Settings* will ensure that all of the changes you have made are reversed, leaving the normal default settings. You can also click the *Tips* button, available on each page, to see a set of hints that are separately dealt with at the end of this chapter.

- The Mouse settings are designed to work with the standard Microsoft mouse driver, but you can encounter problems if you have them applied to any other driver. In particular, if you use a trackball that is not of Microsoft manufacture, you should not use the Mouse settings of TweakUI. As a precaution, save your Registry before using TweakUI.

## General

The General panel starts with a set of items marked as *Effects*. Each item has a check box so that you can select any one or any combination as you wish, and each logged user can make his/her separate settings.

The item marked *Window animation* deals with the animation effects that you can see when you minimise, maximise, or restore a window. Leave this unchecked if you prefer the faster changes that you get without animation. For Windows 98 there is also a *Smooth scrolling* option for animated window scrolling in Explorer and other programs, and this can be ticked separately.

If you like to hear a sound reminder of errors, you can check the *Beep on errors* item. The sound that is used can be selected using the *Sounds* item on the Control Panel. The three items that follow enable animation of *Menu*, *Combo box* and *List box* respectively and once again, you can tick separate boxes to select these effects. Remember that animated displays use processor time, and so slow down the overall action of your computer.

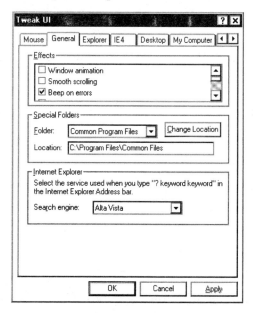

The *Menu underline* item can be ticked to ensure that on each menu that you see, the underlined letter(s) will indicate a keyboard shortcut. The check box following this is labelled *X-Mouse Autoraise*, and **if** your computer supports the action, it will ensure that placing the mouse pointer on a window not only makes this the active window but also makes it the top window that you can see over all others.

The item marked *Mouse hot-tracking effects* allows the use of actions such as *ToolTips*, and you should not need to use this because Windows 98 will enable this as a default. If, however, you cannot use these effects, try ticking the check box. You can also opt to *Show Windows version on desktop* if you make use of the desktop and want a reminder of the version number.

The second part of the General panel is labelled *Special Folders*, and it allows you to change the locations of the following folders that are reserved for special purposes:

| | |
|---|---|
| Common program files | Desktop |
| Document templates | Favorites |
| My documents | Program files |
| Programs | Recent documents |
| Send To | Start Menu |
| Startup | |

You can select the folder from the list that you will see when you click the arrowhead, and change the location by clicking the *Change Location* button. The change will take place when you restart or log on again, and each user can select individual settings. You should not alter these settings, however, unless you particularly need to.

The last portion of this panel decides which of the common search engines of the Internet you use when you type a search using the **?** format in the address bar of Explorer. For example, if you typed **? Costa Rica** to find information about Costa Rica, you might want to specify which search engine was used in preference, based on your experience of which serves your needs best. My own favourite is Alta Vista, but the searches you make might be better served by another from the list, which typically contains:

| | |
|---|---|
| Alta Vista | Custom |
| Excite | HotBot |
| Infoseek | Infoseek Ultra |
| Lycos | Magellan |
| Metacrawler | Open Text |
| Web Crawler | Yahoo |

If you select *Custom*, you will be asked to type in the URL (address) for a site that is not on the list. Each user of your computer can specify a different search engine.

**Explorer**

This panel uses three sections, *Shortcut overlay*, *Startup* and *Settings*, all relating to Windows Explorer. *Shortcut overlay* allows you to choose how Explorer indicates that an icon represents a shortcut. You can choose from *Arrow* (the default), *Light arrow*, *None* or *Custom*. If you choose the *Custom* setting you will see a variety of styles and you can browse for others if you know what file contains them. Whatever setting is used will apply to all users of your computer.

The second section allows you to determine whether or not you use the *Click here to begin* box on the taskbar when you start Windows (or log in as a new user), and whether or not to use the *Tip of the Day* feature. As for most TweakUI settings, each user can create his/her settings separately.

## Understanding Windows 98 Registry

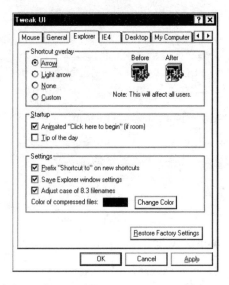

In the *Settings* section, the first item is *Prefix Shortcut to*, and checking this box has the effect of putting the phrase 'shortcut to' to indicate a new shortcut. The box labelled *Save Explorer window settings* can be checked to save the settings of the Explorer window for a folder when you close it. The next time you run Explorer, your settings will be restored. The last setting in this set is labelled *Adjust case of 8.3 filenames* and when this box has been checked, the MS-DOS type of all-uppercase filenames will be converted to mixed case. For example, a name such as MYFILES.DOC will be converted to Myfiles.doc. The panel ends with a *Change Color* button. This applies when you use compressed files and have configured Explorer to show these in a different colour. You can click the button to change the default colour for compressed files.

For all of these settings, each user can make his/her own selection. The *Restore Factory Settings* button can be clicked to reverse all the changes you have made in this set.

## IE4

The list of choices in this panel applies to Internet Explorer 4 as supplied with Windows 98, and the arrival of IE5 later in 1999 may affect the action of some of these choices. IE5 has a rather different look and feel, and if you upgrade Windows 98 to incorporate IE5 you might feel that you do not need the IE4 tweaks.

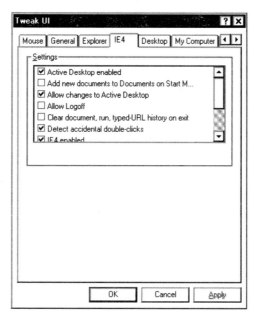

The first item is *Active Desktop enabled*, and this will be ticked if you have already selected this option elsewhere. This box provides a simple way of enabling and disabling this feature. The next item is *Add new documents to Documents on Start Menu*, and if you clear the tick on this one, your Documents list will unaffected by your IE4 use (though it will still show other documents used by other programs). The following item of *Allow changes to Active Desktop* must be ticked if you want to see the options for altering the *Active Desktop* settings.

# Understanding Windows 98 Registry

The box labelled *Allow Logoff* will affect the *Log off* item on the Start — Shut down menu. Tick the box to make this item appear, clear the box if you do not need to have different users logging on and off. You can tick the *Clear document, run, typed-URL history on exit* if you want the items to be erased when you log off, so that the next user does not see your additions to the *Document Run history* and URL addresses that you have typed. With this box cleared, these items are retained for all users.

The *Detect accidental double-clicks* box should be ticked, because this ensures that double-clicking in IE4 is ignored. If you clear this box, any double-click you make is likely to be treated as two separate single clicks, so that you could start two copies of a Web site. The *IE4 enabled* box ensures that you retain the distinctive appearance of Internet Explorer 4, and clearing the box will make the IE4 of Windows 98 look like the Windows 95 type of display.

The last two items deal with sections of the Start menu which you can hide or make visible. Tick the *Show Documents on Start Menu* item if you want to see the Documents item appearing in the Start menu. You can similarly enable or disable the appearance of the *Favorites* item in the Start menu.

Lastly, you can opt for *Show Internet Icon* on desktop, and you should ensure that this box is ticked even if you never use the Internet icon on your Desktop. If you clear this box it has the side effect that the *Windows Update* item in the Start menu will not operate and will show a *file not found* type of error message when clicked. You can still get to Windows Update by using the URL of:

http://windowsupdate.microsoft.com/default.htm

in the normal way.

**Desktop**

This panel deals with icons that can be placed on the Desktop, though the list includes at least two items (Control Panel and Printers) that cannot be placed on the Desktop. You will also find that Internet Explorer appears on the list (possibly more than once), conflicting with the setting in the previous panel. If no checkbox appears next to an item then the icon cannot be placed on the desktop (but see later for creating a file).

You can tick a box to add a desktop icon or you can clear the box to remove that icon from the desktop. As noted earlier, you should not remove Internet Explorer from your desktop, but if you have ticked this option in the IE4 set you do not need to have the box ticked in this set. You may also encounter problems if you remove some other icons, such as Network Neighborhood (even if you do not use a network). Removing an icon affects only a shortcut and does not remove program software.

## Understanding Windows 98 Registry

Icons, such as those for Printers, that have no check-box cannot be placed on the desktop as special desktop icons. You can use the *Create As File* button to put a shortcut on the desktop or in any folder. The options of *Show on desktop*, *Create as file* and *Rename* appear when you right-click any item.

The desktop icons appear for all users, with the exception of *Network Neighborhood* which can be enabled or disabled for each individual user. Altering this icon has no effect until you have logged off and then logged on again.

The items that, typically, appear in the list are:

| | |
|---|---|
| ActiveX Cache Folder | Control Panel |
| Dial-up Networking | Inbox |
| Internet Cache Folder | Internet Explorer |
| Network Neighborhood | Printer |
| Recycle Bin | Scheduled Tasks |
| Shell Favorite Folder | Subscriptions Folder |
| The Internet | The Microsoft Network |
| URL History folder | |

### My Computer

This panel shows a list of drives, and you can click on a check-box for any drive, if it exists, to enable or disable the display in My Computer. The default is to show all drives from A: to Z: enabled, and you should not normally alter this.

- If you disable drive letters you may find that right-clicking the Start button no longer offers the usual range of menu options.

**Control Panel**

When you click this tab, you will see a list of the items in your Control Panel, along with the filename for each. Inevitably, in any Control Panel list there will be some items that you never use. These files, with the CPL extension letters, are normally located in the C:\Windows\System folder, but you can enable or disable each by using this panel rather then by using the older method of moving unwanted files to another folder. A typical list is:

| *Filename* | *Effect* |
|---|---|
| access.cpl | Windows Accessibility options |
| appwiz.cpl | Add/Remove programs |
| desk.cpl | Desktop settings |
| findfast.cpl | Control FindFast action |
| inetcpl.cpl | Internet controls |
| intl.cpl | Regional settings |
| menu.cpl | Mouse, keyboard, etc. |
| mmsys.cpl | Multimedia |
| modem.cpl | Modem setup |
| netcpl.cpl | Network setup |
| powercfg.cpl | Power management |
| sysdm.cpl | System controls |
| telephon.cpl | Windows Telephony |
| timdate.cpl | Time and Date settings |
| tweakui.cpl | The TweakUI settings |

## Understanding Windows 98 Registry

### Network

The Network panel is useful only if you are connected to a network using Microsoft Networking and you want to automate your logging on. You can tick the box marked *Log on automatically at system startup* so that your name and password is entered automatically. You can override this setting temporarily by holding down the Shift key as you start up the computer. This setting applies to all users. You are warned that the name and password used here is not encrypted and can be read from the registry files.

### New

The New list shows a set of document types (templates) that are currently used on your computer. The boxes that are ticked indicate the options that are available when you use File — New or right-click on a folder name in the right-hand side of an Explorer display and select *New*. The list will usually include Microsoft Word Document and Text Document, and other types according to your software.

You can remove a template by selecting and clicking the *Remove* button — note that some types cannot be removed. You can add another template to this list by dragging a file using the template into this window.

### Add/Remove

When you click on this tab you will see the current list that appears in the *Add/Remove* panel of Control Panel. You can right-click any entry to see a menu of *Edit*, *Remove* or *Rename*, and the *Edit* and *Remove* items are also obtainable from buttons. If you use *Remove*, the item is removed from the list, but this does not alter any software, it simple makes it impossible to uninstall the item using the Add/Remove feature.

The *New* button allows you to create a new entry, but only if you know what to specify. A panel appears calling for entries under the headings of *Description* and *Command*. The *Description* portion is the name of the program as it should appear in the Add/Remove panel, and the *Command* line contains the path of the program file for uninstalling the program. For example, the item called Microsoft Outlook Express uses the *Command line*:

C:\Program Files\Outlook Express\_isetup.exe
/UNINSTALL/PROMPT

This provides a way of restoring an item to the list, but there is no point in trying to add an item for which you do not know an UNINSTALL location. You can use the *Edit* action to see what command is used for each of your existing entries.

**Boot**

The Boot panel deals with actions that affect how Windows 98 boots up. The first option is marked *Function keys available* and the (default) tick on this box allows you to interrupt the boot action by pressing the various functions keys such as F5 and F8. Test to see if your computer responds to those keys or uses the Ctrl key instead for Windows 98. Remove the tick on the box if you want the boot action to be unaffected by the Function keys.

The option marked *Start GUI automatically* is normally ticked, and if you remove the tick the computer will hang up when it has loaded MS-DOS, waiting for the command to start Windows. The *Display splash screen* option can be used to disable the 'Starting Windows 98' screen that appears during booting. This allows you to see the log of actions that have been carried out so far, and can be useful for troubleshooting. It also saves a small amount of time during booting.

## Understanding Windows 98 Registry

If you installed Windows 98 without removing its predecessor (Windows 95 or Windows 3.1) you can opt to use the F4 key to select the older system when you are booting up. This will have no effect if you installed Windows 98 over the older system or if you have deleted files from the older system.

The item marked *Always show boot menu* is normally unchecked but you can tick this box if you want to see the boot menu (such as you see when you hold down the Ctrl key as you boot Windows 98) each time you start Windows. This can be useful during troubleshooting. If this box is not ticked a boot menu will appear only if there was a problem on the previous boot. You can choose for yourself using the *Continue booting after nn seconds* box how long you want the boot menu to remain on screen before it starts Windows 98 automatically.

The box marked *Autorun Scandisk* controls the use of Scandisk when Windows is booted after having been shut down prematurely. The normal default is After prompting, but you can opt for *Never* or *Without prompting*. This panel also uses a *Restore Factory Settings* button.

### Repair

The Repair panel is concerned with repairing files that are liable to be damaged by the installation of new programs. The full list is:

Rebuild Icons      Repair Associations

Repair Font Folder      Repair Regedit

Repair System Files      Repair Temporary Internet Files

Repair URL History

The *Rebuild Icons* action can be clicked to rebuild all the Explorer icons and to remove unused Explorer icons from the memory. You would normally use this if you found that

Explorer was displaying the wrong icon for a program or a shortcut.

The item listed as *Repair Associations* will returns icons to their original settings and also restores the default associations for standard file types such as DOC. TXT, etc. You will need to use this action if you find that you no longer see an *Install* option when you right-click an information (INF) file so as to install a program.

The option for *Rebuild Font Folder* should be used if you find that the C:\Windows\Fonts folder is displaying like an ordinary folder, with no access to menu actions such as *Install New Font, List Fonts by Similarity* and so on. The *Repair Regedit* item needs to be used if you find that when you run *regedit* it does not show its normal set of columns.

The item marked *Repair system files* will check files that are liable to be replaced by installing other programs. Windows will restore the original version if it finds that any important file has been replaced. You should, in particular, run this action if you start to get the error message:

The Comdlg32.dll file cannot start.

This action cannot be used unless the files in the folder C:\Windows\SysBckup are still installed. This folder may be hidden, so you have to opt to see hidden files in your Explorer File — Folder Options — View menu.

The *Temporary Internet Files* item is needed if you find that you can no longer see the columns marked *Internet Address* and *Expires* when you view the C:\Windows\Temporary Internet Files folder. Similarly, the *URL History* item will be needed if you cannot see the columns of *Last Visited* and *Expires* when you view the C:\Windows\History folder and use *Details* view.

## Understanding Windows 98 Registry

### Paranoia

The *Paranoia* panel is used to ensure peace of mind regarding the record of what you did and what can happen without notification. In particular, it concentrates on removing any data logs that reveal to another user what you have been doing.

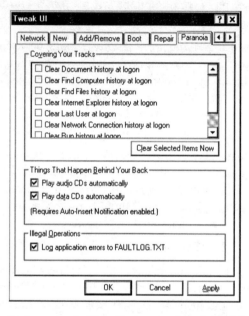

The section marked *Covering your tracks* will erase any records of files, folders and Web sites that you have visited. The list of items covered by this consists of history logs for:

| | |
|---|---|
| Documents | Find Computer |
| Find Files | Internet Explorer |
| Last User | Network Connection |
| Run | Telnet |

Note that the *Run history* item refers only to Explorer, and does not cover the *Run history* item of other programs such as Norton Navigator.

The second section is titled *Things that happen behind your back*, and it concerns the use of the CD-ROM drive. You can opt to enable or disable *Play audio CDs automatically* and *Play data CDs automatically* using the check boxes in this section.

The last section contains only *Log application errors to FAULTLOG.TXT*, and you will probably want to tick this box so that you see this file and find a record of these errors.

## Tips section

The Tips section of TweakUI contains some useful tips that you will probably find elsewhere also, but which are certain to be new to a large number of readers. These are summarised below.

## Default extensions

Normally an application uses a default extension for its files, such as DOC for Word files. You can dispense with the addition of a default extension if you place quotes around the filename, so that using "Myfile.last" will ensure that this file is recorded as Myfile.last rather than as Myfile.last.doc.

## Desktop clutter

If you feel that your desktop is too cluttered, you can use TweakUI to remove icons or convert these icons into files that you can place in folders. You are warned that some icons will not behave well when converted into files in this way.

## Hiding desktop icons

If other people use your computer, you can hide some desktop icons from them provided they log in separately.

# Understanding Windows 98 Registry

You can then delete some icons from their desktop, but restore them on your own private version.

### Special icons onto the Start Menu

Start TweakUI and go to Desktop. Select Control Panel and click the Create As File button. When you see the Explorer type of view of folders and files, find C:\Windows\Start Menu and select this folder for the Control Panel file. This will add the Control Panel item just under Windows Update and you can place the pointer on the small triangle to open up a list of Control Panel options. You can remove this by deleting the file from C:\Windows\Start Menu. You can use this system also for Printers and Dial-Up Networking.

### Troubleshooters

Start TweakUI and click the *Tips* button on the *Mouse* panel. Click on *Troubleshooting* to find troubleshooting hints for creating a template, display of unwanted folders when Explorer starts, and a 'See also' set.

### Consequences of hiding Network Neighborhood

This part discusses why you should not hide the Network Neighborhood icon, since it will affect your ability to use Explorer and also has an odd effect on Direct Cable Connection.

## Registry editing

Many of the alterations that you see recommended and might want to try are provided only by directly editing the Registry, rather than through TweakUI or the Control Panel, and two golden rules apply here.

> 1. Do not tweak at random. Either follow a recommended procedure (from a book or magazine) or carry out an edit that changes a value in a way that you believe will be acceptable.

2. Always, always, make a separate backup using the Export action of *regedit* before you alter any part of the Registry. Remember that the effects of your editing may not show up immediately, by which time all of the automatic Registry backups will contain the changes.

You neglect this advice at your own risk. Windows is a very complicated system, and there are depths that very few have ever plumbed. Don't expect any sympathy from Microsoft's help line (if you can get in touch) if you have experienced problems after altering the Registry. The best you can hope for is that there will be an article in the Microsoft knowledge base — but if your computer isn't working you can't look up the knowledge base.

## Editing the Registry

Registry editing can be done using *regedit*, and though there are other Registry editors available, we'll illustrate the use of *regedit* because it is provided as part of Windows 98. The two most important sections of the Registry from the point of view of making tweaks are HKEY_CURRENT_USER and HKEY_LOCAL_MACHINE. If you are a single user, not sharing the PC and not on a network, these are the only sections in which you are ever likely to make tweaks.

The use of *regedit* for altering the Registry is best illustrated by a concrete example, and we'll look at how to alter some of the data that the computer holds on you, the owner of the computer.

Begin by clicking the Start button, and then Run. Fill in the name regedit into the panel that appears (if it is not already there) and click the OK button. This should bring up the Registry editor panel as illustrated.

# Understanding Windows 98 Registry

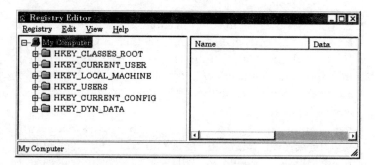

You should now use the Registry — Export menu item to make a backup that is separate from the daily backup set. Make sure that this backup is placed in a folder that you can get at if you need to restore the Registry.

The section that you need to use to make the example tweak is:

HKEY_LOCAL_MACHINE

and you need to move the cursor to the [+] box at the left-hand side of the folder icon with this name.

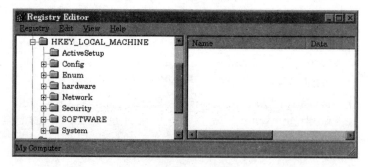

Click on this box to reveal the next layer, and then on the [+] box labelled *software*. Books and magazine articles often show this type of step in the form:

Hkey_Local_Machine/software

and finding a line to edit will usually involve clicking on a number of the [+] boxes in turn.

In this example, after clicking on the [+] sign for *software*, find the *Microsoft* entry, click on its box, then find *Windows*, click on this, then *current version*. This whole process can be written as:

Hkey_Local_machine/software/Microsoft/Windows/current version.

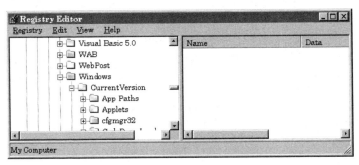

Now click on the current version name. This is a key name, and you will now see in the right-hand panel the data that belongs to this key. Scroll down to find the *RegisteredOwner* entry. You can now edit this to whatever you like, and also if you want, add something for the companion *RegisteredOrganization* entry. The *ProductKey* entry, incidentally, shows the key code that you had to use to confirm use of the installation CD-ROM, so that if you did not make a note of the key earlier you can do so now.

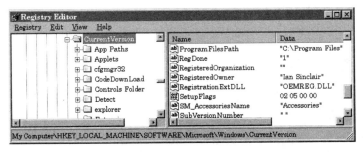

## Understanding Windows 98 Registry

How do you alter the data? Click on the name of the key, in this example, *RegisteredOwner*, so that it appears selected. Now click the Edit menu, and click on the first item, *Modify*.

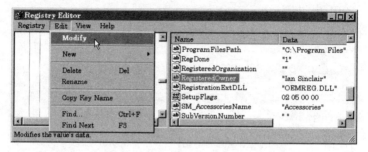

You will now see a separate editing panel appear, and you can delete the name in this panel and substitute what you want.

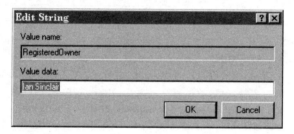

After that, just click the *OK* keys until you can leave the editor. From now on, where the name of the user appears in a form it will show the name you have edited into this space. You do not, needless to say, have to use your own name and if you want to answer to names like *Zorro the Zilch* then that's up to you.

- Remember that if anything nasty happens (and it is not unknown for the electricity supply to fail while you are altering the Registry) you can use the backup you made to restore things just as they were.

- Once you have opened a new layer by clicking the [+] box you can close it again by clicking the [-] box.

You do not need to close all the layers before leaving *regedit*, because they will be closed automatically.

## Some recommended tweaks

Recommending a tweak is always a very personal matter, because what one user considers as a very satisfying tweak is a total irrelevance to another. Remember that you can carry out a large amount of tweaking without any direct editing of the Registry by using the TweakUI Control Panel item from the Resource Kit.

What follows are some well-known tweaks that apply to Windows 98, and most of them are also applicable to Windows 95. There are some tweaks that you will see in magazine pages and on Net pages that are applicable to Windows 95 only. This is because Windows 98 uses a few different methods, and you should be careful about trying out any older Windows 95 Registry tweaks on a machine that is running Windows 98. The usual result is that the tweak simply does nothing, but you might not be so lucky.

- Be particularly careful about tweaks that involve typing a completely new key name. Several of these tweaks are known for Windows 95, but the action has subsequently been incorporated into Windows 98 in a different way.

- Don't forget the backups!

## Default Search engine

If you have used several search engines you will by this time have formed an opinion on your favourite. You can make this the default search engine that Explorer will open when you select Find — On the Internet from the Start menu.

First, you must find and note carefully the address (the URL) of your favourite search engine — this is likely to be a long address and you must copy it exactly. Now run *regedit* and

# Understanding Windows 98 Registry

click in turn on: HKEY_CURRENT_USER, Software, Microsoft, Internet Explorer, Main key. You will see a long list of items in the right hand side of the display. Double-click on the one named *SearchPage* and when the *Edit String* panel opens, copy the address for your search engine into the *Value Data* box.

- If you alter the address in *SearchBar* (just above *SearchPage*) this will change the URL that is obtained when you click on the Search icon in the main toolbar.

- If you use a link on the Link bar, remember that you can right-click the link and edit the name of the URL that it will connect to.

## Download path

When you download a file from the Internet you are likely to find that the default path is to the floppy drive. This is a precaution against a virus-corrupted file getting into your hard drive, and you can run a virus check on the file on your floppy before you copy it to the hard drive. You can, however, use any other folder if you want. This includes a CD-R or CD-RW drive if you want to store large files on a CD-ROM.

If you want to download, as a default, to another path such as C:\Download, you can alter the Registry entry that contains the path description. Click Start — Run and launch *regedit*.

Click the [+] box next to HKEY_CURRENT_USER. Now click in the boxes for *Software*, *Microsoft* and then click on the name *Internet explorer*. You will see on the right-hand side the *DownloadDirectory* name, and the *Data* value "A:\". Click on *DownloadDirectory* and then click Edit — Modify. In the panel that appears, edit the A:\ name to any other folder description such as C:\Download. Note that you do not need to type the inverted commas.

Now exit from *regedit*, re-boot, and you are ready to make use of the altered default download path.

## Multiple extensions

The usual action of the View — Folder options — File types panel is to allow you to associate a program with an extension, so that, for example, the txt extension is associated with NotePad. Once an association is made, you can click on a file with the txt extension so that NotePad will open with the file loaded in.

It's quite a different matter if you want to use more than one extension for a program. In some cases this is not feasible because of conflicts — there is nothing in Windows that would allow it to choose which of two programs to use if they were both associated with the same extension. The usual way of setting up multiple extensions is to click on a file that has the new extension you want to associate, and then select the program that you want to use for it from the list that appears. You can, however, add a Registry entry that will add this extension so that it is associated with an existing program. The simplest example to use is associating ME with NotePad, so that clicking on a READ.ME file will open Notepad with the file loaded in.

To start with, check that this association has not already been made. Use View — Folder options — File types to look for the Text Document type, and read the Extension list that appears. This will start with TXT and you may also find EXC and DIC as well. If ME does not appear, you can now add it by editing the Registry.

Backup, then use *regedit* to open HKEY_CLASSES_ROOT. Look at the entry for TXT, and you will find that the default setting is *txtfile*. Now select HKEY_CLASSES_ROOT and click Edit — New — Key. You will see a box appear at the end of the left-hand panel with a name such as *New Key #1*, and you can edit this to the extension that you want to use,

# Understanding Windows 98 Registry

.ME in this example (don't forget the dot). You will not be allowed to enter any extension that already exists in the list. Press the Return key to create this new key.

Now move to the right-hand panel where the line:

(Default)     (value not set)

appears. Click on (Default) and then on the Edit menu. Click on Modify to see the window in which you can enter the word *txtfile* as the default value. Leave the editing action and shut down *regedit*.

From now on, you will see .ME as one of the list of extensions in the *Text Document* type of File Types.

## Start menu speed

The speed at which your Start menu operates is controlled by a Registry setting. Start in HKEY_CURRENT_USER and go to Control Panel/desktop. With *desktop* highlighted, you will see a set of data items on the right-hand side. Look for the one called *MenuShowDelay*. You may find that this is a value of 17. Change it to something smaller, between 1 and 10, to make your Start menu move faster.

## Windows Setup path

When you installed Windows 98 you probably use the CD-ROM as the source of the files. You may not have realised that you can copy all of the CAB files on the CD-ROM onto your hard drive. You can, for example, create and use a folder called C:\CABfile for this purpose.

The advantage is that if you frequently want to use the Setup program to alter your Windows, you need not use the CD-ROM again. You will, however, be asked to put the CD-ROM into its drive or specify a place where the files can be read unless you alter the Registry so that your folder is given as the default place to read these files.

## Registry tweaks

Go to HKEY_LOCAL_MACHINE and follow the path:

Software/Microsoft/Windows/CurrentVersion/Setup

Click on *Setup* and in the list of data that appears in the right-hand panel, find the one called *SourcePath*. This will have a data value of "D:\Win98\". Edit this value to whatever you have used, such as "C:\CABfile" and enter this. Now when you use Setup it will use the CAB files on the hard drive automatically.

# 5 Disaster recovery

## Don't panic!

It's easy enough to say, because when you see the pointer disappear, and find that no key has any effect on the screen, your first natural response **is** to panic, even if you know that you have a good set of backups. This situation is called a *lockout* or *lockup*, and newcomers to computing are always worried that there will be some sort of mechanical damage and that they will have to replace the computer. This is, in fact, the least likely eventuality, and unless you can hear nasty grinding sounds (or total silence), or see smoke coming from the casing, mechanical damage is not high on the list.

In the event of a lockout, the first thing to try is to press the Alt–Ctrl–Del keys together. If the computer is responding in any way the keyboard this is likely to bring up a little box with a list of programs.

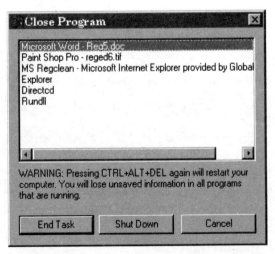

The top item will be highlighted, and if you see a message to the effect that this program is not responding, you can click the *End Task* button so as to shut down this program, leaving everything else running. This allows you to get on with working, and you can restart the program that caused the problem.

- Sometimes Word can cause such a lockout, and the fault is not in Windows or in Word itself but in the document template. The remedy is to note the layout of that template, delete it, and create a new version.

The worst lockouts, however, often disable the keyboard as well, so that no key or key combination has any effect. In this case, all you can do is to switch off. You can now thank your lucky stars that you took my advice and made a backup of the Registry, or, possibly, hope that one of the automatic backups will restore things. What you cannot do is to restart and hope that the problems will go away, because a total lockup is often caused by a Registry fault, and it will not go away until the Registry is changed.

You must therefore go through the standard Windows 98 rescue routine:

1. Switch on, and hold down the F8 key (or left-hand Ctrl key) until you see the boot menu appear.

2. Select the Safe Command Mode option

3. With MS-DOD running, type the command:

scanreg /backup

and when the list of backup files appears, select one from a day when the Registry gave no problems. It's often advisable if you have not changed hardware or software to select the oldest version.

4. Start the restoration, and when the MS-DOS prompt returns, shut down.

5.  Allow a few minutes and then restart, this time allowing Windows to start normally.

## Corrupt backups

The system of multiple backups that Windows 98 uses is proof against several types of hang-up, but it can be sabotaged by your own actions. One certain way is to keep re-booting and reproducing the fault for several days running. This ensures that all of your backup copies are equally corrupted. Another equally bad option is to use the Tools to make several new backups in one day, which can also result in all of the copies being corrupted.

This need not be a worry if you have made a copy, earlier, using the *Export* command of *regedit*. You do not need to do this very often, and you would normally make such a backup just before you installed a new hardware item or a new piece of software. You might make another such backup once you were convinced that your new hardware or software was working flawlessly. You can restore from such a copy with no worries.

The trouble is that you need to have either MS-DOS or Windows working before you can use *regedit* easily. To ensure that Windows will work smoothly, you should use the F8 (or left-hand Ctrl) key option again, and select item 3, *Safe mode* to start Windows. This will use the bare minimum of drivers to start Windows with minimal resources, but you can use Start — Run and so enter *regedit*.

With this running, you can use the File — Import command to locate and load one of your exported backup files. Once this has replaced the old Registry, and can use Start — Shut down and then *Restart*, this time leaving Windows to load by itself in its normal mode.

The last possible thing to contemplate is re-installing Windows. This can be a very long drawn out business (even if you can copied the CAB files to the hard drive), and you may find that you then have to install other hardware and software all over again. The only fault-chasing reasons for taking these drastic steps are that all your normal Registry automatic backups are corrupt, the *scanreg /fix* utility cannot repair any of them, and you have never created any exported REG files.

The other reason for a complete re-installation is if you have decided to shuffle hard drives around. Suppose you have a large hard drive installed, and a spare smaller one not doing anything useful. You might think, correctly, that you could with advantage use the smaller drive as the C:\ drive, holding MS-DOS and Windows files only, and keep the large drive for other programs and for data.

It's all quite true, and Windows will run fast from a defragmented small drive, but getting to this stage is a very awkward business. You have to disconnect the existing C: drive and connect it to the other data connector so that the small drive can be connected in its place. You need to format the small drive and install Windows on it. You now have two copies of Windows (one on each drive) and two Registry file sets, and you must make certain that the Windows files on the second drive are deleted. You then have to re-install all your hardware and software, because the new Registry has no data about a second hard drive being present. There are programs available to do all this, and unless you want to do it all the hard way, it's much better to take all the help you can get.

# Appendix A

## Sources for registry hints and tips

Your main sources for hints and tips on Registry alterations are magazines, and also Web pages. Magazines are a pretty reliable source of Registry information, and you can be fairly certain that any Registry tip that you see published will have been checked out on several computers. If you want to be thoroughly safe, check with later volumes of the magazine concerned to find if there are any letters from readers that indicate problems with a Registry edit.

Internet recommendations are a shade more risky unless they come from a source that you know is reliable. Provided that you keep good backups, however, it is most unlikely that you would run into trouble by following a hint. The thing to avoid is downloading any software that will modify the Registry, and which might contain a virus. Once again, you have to use some discretion, and trust some providers more than others.

A few Web sites that I have found useful are listed below. This is not a guarantee that the information is flawless, but I have checked several of the tweaks and found no problems.

One highly recommended source of information is Ron Badour's page on:

http://mbr-hobby.neotown.com/rwbadour/index.html

Ron Badour's name crops up in several Newsgroups, answering queries that have stumped other services. His Web pages are a mine of information on Windows and other Microsoft systems.

Jolly's Windows Registry is another source of information and has the unusual Web URL of http://start.at/windowsregistry

The page called Windows 98 Tweaks is yet another of many devoted to Registry editing, and is at:

http://win98central.acauth.com/win98/regtweaks.htm

Simon Clausen's site is another useful source of information, frequently updated, and is at:

http://www.regedit.com

You can also register for emailed updates.

These are all recommended sources of information, and are updated regularly. You can find others by making a search for "Windows 98 registry", but some are not what they seem and are concerned mainly with Windows 95 tips.

- Remember that if you search for Windows 98 registry (with no quotes) you will get pages that contain any one of these words. This makes the list too long, and containing too much that is not relevant.

# Appendix B

## Other registry tools

Many registry tools are shareware, so that they are offered on the basis that you try them out and pay if you find them useful. These programs do not have the background of extensive testing that you expect of a commercial product, and they may have very little in the way of documentation or assistance. That said, some are very well designed products and they provide an answer to problems that are more difficult to solve using commercial software.

Registry tools are classed as utilities, and can be downloaded from various Web sites. One that has a good selection of Registry tools is on the ZDNet site at:

http://www.zdnet.com/anchordesk/story/story_2755.html

You can also find good shareware by searching through the items on the site:

http://davecentral.com/

and another source of freeware and shareware is:

http://www.datascribe.com.au/mirrors/nonags/index.html

Remember once again that you cannot ever take the Registry on trust – always made backups before you use any software that affects the Registry.

# Appendix C

## Code numbers

The following is a list of code numbers that are used in place of filenames for various items that appear on the Desktop and as references in the Registry. You will not need these if you are not deleting these items from the Registry, but you certainly will if you have already deleted some item and cannot find how to restore it.

Control Panel

{21EC2020-3AEA-1069-A2DD-08002B30309D}

Printers

{2227A280-3AEA-1069-A2DE-08002B30309D}

Recycle Bin

{645FF040-5081-101B-9F08-00AA002F954E}

My Computer

{20D04FE0-3AEA-1069-A2D8-08002B30309D}

Dial-Up Networking & Network Neighborhood

{208D2C60-3AEA-1069-A2D7-08002B30309D}

Inbox

{00020D75-0000-0000-C000-000000000046}

Desktop

{00021400-0000-0000-C000-000000000046}

Shortcut

{00021401-0000-0000-C000-000000000046}

# INDEX

? icon.................................. 40
[+] symbol.......................... 9

*Active Desktop enabled*.... 47
Add/Remove tab .............. 52
*Adjust case of 8.3
    filenames* ...................... 46
*Allow Logoff*.................... 48
Alt–Ctrl–Del keys............. 68
*Always show boot menu*... 54
animation, boxes .............. 43
attributes .......................... 24
automatic backing up....... 11
*Autorun Scandisk*............. 54

backup............................ 1, 5
backup copies corrupted .. 70
backup directory .............. 17
backup whole registry...... 19
binary values..................... 7
bloated Registry ............... 27
Boot tab............................ 53

CAB files ..................... 5, 11
cascading menu speed...... 40
CD-ROM drive ................ 57
CFGBACK.EXE............... 25
*change files* option ........... 36
*Change Location* button .. 44
code numbers .................... 75
Command mode............... 14
comment line .................... 16
comment, backup............. 14
compacting....................... 16
compacting Registry .. 13, 27

conflict................................6
contents of CAB file.........18
Control Panel......................2
Control Panel tab..............51
*Copy* command.................19
corrupted Registry ............15
*Covering your tracks*........56
CPL extension ,................51
*Create As File*....................50

DA0 files ...........................21
data entry ............................9
database ..............................2
default extension ..............57
default search engine........63
defragmentation................27
de-installation ....................3
desktop clutter ..................57
Desktop tab.......................49
*Detect accidental double-
    clicks* ...............................48
directly editing Registry ...58
disaster recovery...............68
*Display splash screen*.......53
display, regedit ...................9
distance between clicks ....41
DLL files ...........................28
*Document Run history*......48
Documents list...................47
*double-click sensitivity* .....41
download path ...................64
*drag sensitivity* ..................41
Dword values......................7

editing Registry ..................1

editing the Registry.......... 39
empty spaces, Registry .... 27
*End Task* .......................... 69
ERU utility...................... 26
example, regedit.............. 59
Explorer tab ..................... 45
Export action...................... 6
exported text files ............ 11
extensions ........................ 65
*Extract* command............. 19

faulty driver ....................... 6
file association types.......... 7
file associations................. 2
file size, Registry ............. 27
files location...................... 4
*Find file errors* action...... 37
*Find, regedit* ..................... 28
*Fix errors* button.............. 30
floppy drive...................... 64
*Function keys available* ... 53

General tab....................... 42

help-line ............................ 1
hide desktop icons............ 57
hierarchical structure ......... 7
hives,................................. 7

*IE4 enabled* ...................... 48
IE4 tab.............................. 47
incorrect Registry............... 2
INI files ............................. 3
installing hardware............. 1

Jolly's Windows Registry 72

keys .................................... 7
keys interchanged ............ 23

large Registry ....................3
list of drives......................50
location for backup files...20
location, CAB files.............6
loudspeaker icon...............36

main sections.....................7
manual checking...............12
mechanical damage ..........68
*Menu underline* ...............43
Microsoft Backup.............12
mouse driver.....................42
mouse tab..........................40
MS-DOS............................22
multiple backing up............5
My Computer tab .............50

nesting ................................3
Net recommendations.......72
network...............................3
Network Neighborhood....49
Network tab.......................52
Network Viewer
      problems ......................32
new association ..................7
new key name...................63
New tab .............................52
number of backups ...........16
numbers .............................7

OLE information ................7
options, SCANREG .........14
original Registry settings..21
other files backup .............17
other Registry utilities ......33

Paranoia tab......................56
PC setup..............................8
*Perfect Companion*...........33
pixels .................................41

# Understanding Windows 98 Registry

POLICY.POL file .............. 4
pop-down actions ............. 42
post-mortem ...................... 6
preferences ........................ 8

RBBAD.CAB file .............. 6
*Rebuild Font Folder* ........ 55
*Rebuild Icons* ................... 54
reg extension .................... 20
REGCLEAN 4.1a ............. 29
regclean utility .................... 2
regedit ................................ 1
regedit use ................. 19, 59
regedit ................................ 8
*RegisteredOwner* entry .... 61
Registry backup ......... 11, 16
*Registry Checker* .............. 11
Registry checking ............ 30
Registry copies.................... 5
Registry editing................ 59
Registry scanning............. 13
Registry system.................. 3
registry tools .................... 74
Registry tweaking ............ 39
re-installing Windows...... 70
removing application ....... 28
*Repair Associations* ......... 55
*Repair system files* ........... 55
Repair tab........................ 54
repairs on Registry ........... 15
restore action, SCANREG 14
*Restore Factory Settings*.. 42
restoring Registry............... 1
restoring Windows 95
    Registry ...................... 22
Ron Badour's page .......... 72
Run box............................. 9

*safe* mode ............... 5, 22, 70
SCANREG.EXE .............. 13

SCANREG.INI................. 15
SCANREGW.EXE........... 13
scrolling wheel ................ 41
search engines ............ 44, 63
semicolon sign................. 16
sensitivity settings ........... 41
separate backup ................. 6
setup path.......................... 66
shortcut data ...................... 7
*Shortcut overlay* .............. 45
shortcut settings................ 46
shortcut, regedit.................. 9
Simon Clausen's site ........ 73
*Smooth scrolling* option ... 43
*Snapshot* facility .............. 35
sound reminder................. 43
sources, hints and tips ...... 72
*Special Folders*,.............. 44
special icons ..................... 58
*Start GUI automatically*... 53
Start menu speed .............. 66
structure, Registry ............. 3
sub-key ............................... 9
System Policies .................. 2
SYSTEM.1ST ................... 21
SYSTEM.DA0 ..................... 4
SYSTEM.DAT..................... 3
SYSTEM.INI...................... 11
SYSTRAY.EXE................ 36

templates............................ 52
*Temporary Internet Files* .55
text file backup ................. 19
time, booting up ............... 11
*Tips* button....................... 42
Tips section ...................... 57
*Troubleshooting* ............... 58
TweakUI............................. 39

*Undo* file....................... 31, 37

USER.DA0 ........................ 4
USER.DAT ....................... 3
utilities .............................. 29

VB5 supporting files........ 34
view Registry ..................... 8
virus precaution ............... 64
volume control ................. 36

Web sites.......................... 72
well-known tweaks .......... 63
WIN.INI........................... 11

*Window animation* ...........43
Windows 95 backup .........21
Windows 95 duplicate files 4
Windows 98 Tweaks ........73
Windows 2000....................2
*Windows Update* ..............48

*X-Mouse* behaviour ..........42

ZDNet site ........................74
Zip ....................................11

# Notes

# Notes

# Notes